ONE STEP AT A TIME

Gabriel Malca

For permission requests,
write to the author at their email address:

Author: Gabriel Malca
Email: gabriel@malca.me

ISBN: 979-8-90243-555-6

For further information about the author
or their publications,
please contact the author via email.

First Edition: 2026

A series of quiet reflections on growing up, pressure,
and becoming yourself.

For Nataniel, Samuel, Benjamin, and Isaac
I am proud of each of you,
for who you are,
and for who you are becoming.

Nataniel,
you've carried responsibility early.
I hope you keep creating for yourself,
and measure your growth only against who you used to be.

Samuel,
you see the world with curiosity and imagination.
I hope you trust the way you think and feel,
and grow confident in who you already are.

Benjamin,
your heart is loyal and fair.
I hope you stay true to yourself,
and remember that being you is enough.

Isaac,
your joy and warmth bring people together.
I hope you keep laughing, being kind,
and growing in your own time.

This world will try to rush you, compare you,
and tell you who you should be.
I hope you always remember that your life is
yours to shape.

CONTENTS

Chapter 1:
WHAT SCHOOL IS REALLY TRAINING YOU FOR

Let me tell you something most people don't explain very well.

School isn't really about being smart.

I know it looks like it is.

You get grades.

You take tests.

People talk about who's good at school and who isn't.

Sometimes it feels like every assignment is quietly deciding what kind of person you are, like it's keeping score when you're not paying attention.

But that's not what's actually happening.

School is more like a place where you're allowed to practice life before things really count.

Most people don't say that part out loud.

When you're sitting at your desk doing work you don't care about, your mind starts wandering.

Why do I have to do this?

When am I ever going to use this?

Does this even matter?

Those thoughts don't mean you're lazy.

They mean you're thinking.

The answer just isn't what most adults say.

A lot of the time, school isn't trying to teach
you the subject.

It's paying attention to how you deal with things.

How you handle boredom.

How you react when something feels hard.

What you do when you mess up.

What happens when you feel pressure.

Those habits follow you everywhere later.

Think about it like a video game.

At the beginning, the levels aren't that exciting.

You mess up a lot.

You fall into things.

You hit the wrong buttons.

You're not really sure where you're going yet.

But the game doesn't kick you out.

You just respawn.

You try again.

You start learning how things work.

And without noticing, you get better.

The early levels exist so mistakes don't cost much.

School works the same way.

You're learning how to deal with challenges while the stakes
are still low.

Some kids struggle in school.

Other kids do really well and still feel stressed all the time.

Both are dealing with pressure.

If you're always trying to be the best, school can start
to feel heavy.

Every test feels like it matters too much.

Every mistake feels risky.

You stop being curious and start being careful.

You're not learning anymore.

You're protecting yourself.

That's when school stops feeling like practice and starts
feeling like something you're being judged on.

And being judged all the time is exhausting.

Adults sometimes add to this, even when they
don't mean to.

Parents push because they're worried.

They know life can be hard.

They want you to be safe later.

They want you to have choices.

They remember times when things didn't work
    out for them.

They don't want that to happen to you.

So they talk about grades like they're everything.

They're not trying to scare you.

They're reacting to their own fears.

You can understand that without letting it take over
    how you feel.

There isn't one perfect path.

Doing everything right in school doesn't guarantee
    a perfect life.

Doing badly doesn't mean you're stuck.

Life doesn't move in a straight line, even though people like
    to pretend it does.

What school really gives you is proof.

Proof that effort changes you.

Proof that you can handle uncomfortable moments.

Proof that you can have a bad day and still be okay.

That proof stays with you, even when plans change.

And school isn't only about work.

It's also where you learn how people work.

It's where you meet all kinds of kids.

Some you like right away.

Some confuse you.

Some are kind.

Some aren't.

Some are just figuring things out, same as you.

You learn what it feels like to make a friend.

You learn what it feels like to be left out.

You learn what it feels like to laugh with people.

And what it feels like when laughter turns into something
that doesn't feel good anymore.

You learn what happens when you stay quiet to fit in.

You learn what happens when you speak up.

You learn how it feels to try joining a game and
not get picked.

You learn how it feels to introduce yourself and have
someone not really care.

None of that means something is wrong with you.

It means you're learning.

School is one of the only places where you can try things
like that and survive the awkwardness.

You can try a new sport even if you're not good yet.

You can sit with different kids at lunch.

You can talk to someone new at recess.

You can see how it feels to put yourself out there, even if it
doesn't go the way you hoped.

Sometimes you'll be accepted.

Sometimes you won't.

And even when it hurts, it teaches you
something about yourself.

Later, you'll understand why those moments don't matter
as much as they feel like they do right now.

They're not the end of the world.

They're part of learning who you are and what actually
matters to you.

That's why the best way to move through school is with
a beginner mindset.

Beginners expect to mess up.

They try things without needing to be good right away.

They learn faster because they're not pretending
they already know.

School is the perfect place to be new at things.

So instead of watching only your grades, try paying
attention to yourself.

Notice how you talk to yourself when
something goes wrong.

Notice how quickly you give up when
something feels uncomfortable.

Notice how you treat people when there's nothing to gain.

Those habits matter more than any test score.

They're shaping who you're becoming.

School isn't there to decide who you are.

It's there to give you a place to practice becoming someone
    you like being.

Someone who's allowed to try without being perfect.

Someone who can mess up and not fall apart.

Someone who's learning, growing, and figuring things out
    one day at a time.

Once you see school that way, it doesn't feel
    so scary anymore.

It feels like a place where you're allowed to learn how
    to be you.

Chapter 2:
WHY ADULTS PUSH YOU SO HARD

You might have noticed something about adults.

They worry a lot.

Sometimes it feels like they're always telling you what to do, what not to do, and what you should care about. Do your homework. Try harder. Don't mess this up. This matters. Think about your future.

After a while, it can feel like you're being watched all the time.

That can be confusing, especially when you already feel like you're trying.

There's a reason this happens.

Most adults aren't pushing you because they think you're not good enough.

They're pushing you because they're afraid.

When adults were kids, they didn't know how their lives would turn out either. Some of them struggled. Some of them felt lost. Some of them wish they had done things differently. Even the ones who seem confident still carry worries around with them.

They've seen that life doesn't always work out the
  way people hope.

Jobs change.

Plans fall apart.

Things don't always go the way they're supposed to.

So when adults look at you, they're not just seeing who you
  are right now.

They're imagining what might happen later.

That fear makes them hold on tighter than they mean to.

When adults say things like "this is important" or "you
  need to try harder" or "this will matter someday," what
  they usually mean is "I don't want you to struggle the
  way I did."

They're trying to protect you.

Fear doesn't always explain itself very well.

Instead of sounding like care, it often sounds like pressure.

Instead of sounding like trust, it can sound like control.

That doesn't make them bad.

It makes them human.

And this is where things can start to feel heavy.

If you're not careful, their fear can start to feel like your
  job to manage.

You might start thinking you have to be perfect so
  they won't worry.

You might start thinking you can't mess up because it
    will disappoint someone.

Slowly, you begin carrying weight that was never meant
    to be yours.

That's a lot for anyone.

Especially a kid.

You're allowed to care about your parents.

And you're allowed to not live inside their fear at
    the same time.

Growing up works a little differently than people expect.

Adults already had their chance to learn things
    the hard way.

You're still in the middle of learning.

That means you're supposed to try things.

You're supposed to make mistakes.

You're supposed to change your mind.

You're supposed to figure out what feels right for you, not
    just what looks right to someone else.

Parents sometimes forget that learning is messy.

They want to skip the hard parts for you.

But the hard parts are where growth actually happens.

This doesn't mean you ignore adults or stop listening.

It means you learn how to hear what they're really saying
    underneath the words.

Most of the time, what they're really saying is that they
want you to be okay.

You can respect that.

And still remember something important.

Your life isn't a test you're trying to pass for someone else.

It's something you're learning how to live.

As you get older, you'll start to notice something else.

No adult has everything figured out.

They're all just older versions of kids who kept going.

Some learned helpful lessons.

Some are still learning them.

That's normal.

You don't need to have all the answers right now.

You don't need to become who someone else imagined
you would be.

You just need to keep learning, keep trying, and stay honest
with yourself about what feels right.

When adults push you, try to remember this.

They're not measuring your worth.

They're trying, in their own imperfect way, to keep you safe.

You can take the love.

You don't have to take the fear.

And when you do that, growing up starts to feel less like
pressure and more like something you're allowed to
figure out as you go.

18

Chapter 3:
WHAT PARENTS CAN SEE
(AND WHAT THEY CAN'T)

There's something important to understand about parents.

They don't see most of your day.

They don't see you sitting in class trying to focus when your mind wanders.

They don't see you rereading something because it didn't make sense the first time.

They don't see the moment when you almost give up and then decide to keep going anyway.

A lot of the effort happens where no one else can see it.

What parents usually see are the parts that come home.

Grades.

Comments.

Reports.

Comparisons.

Those are the signals they're given.

So that's what they pay attention to.

This isn't because they don't care about you.

It's because they care deeply.

And because life has become complicated.

A long time ago, parents taught their kids
    almost everything themselves.

How to work.

How to behave.

How to solve problems.

How to get along with people.

But as jobs took more time, and life became busier and
    more expensive, that role slowly shifted.

School took over a lot of it.

Parents now have to trust a system they don't control.

They don't get to see what makes sense to you.

They don't get to watch how you're taught.

They don't get to know what works for you
    and what doesn't.

So they look for signs that things are going well.

Grades become one of the few signs they can see.

Not because grades tell the whole story.

But because they're visible.

And parents feel pressure too.

They want to feel like they made good choices.

They want to believe they're doing a good job.

Sometimes they want to feel proud.

Sometimes they want reassurance.

They don't always say this out loud.

But it's there.

If school costs money, that pressure can feel even heavier.

Parents want to believe they chose the right place.

The right program.

The right opportunities.

Good grades feel like confirmation.

Not of you.

But of the choice they made.

None of this means you're failing if you don't fit neatly
into the system.

And none of it is your fault.

School isn't built one way because everyone learns the same.

It's built one way because it's the easiest way to teach a lot
of kids at once.

Some kids fit that system easily.

Some have to work harder to adjust.

Some learn differently.

That doesn't mean one is trying more than another.

It just means people aren't all the same.

When parents don't see effort, they sometimes assume
it isn't there.

Not because they're judging you.

But because effort is hard to measure.

That's why small things can matter more than they seem.

Letting them see you sit down to study.

Asking a question out loud.

Showing that you're trying, even when it's frustrating.

Not to impress them.

But to help them understand what they can't see.

There's something else that matters too.

Respect.

Not the kind that comes from fear.

The kind that comes from noticing.

Your parents are carrying more than you can see.

Work.

Money.

Bills.

Schedules.

Worries.

Plans.

They're thinking about groceries, rent, school, activities,
rides, friendships, and problems you haven't
even noticed yet.

They don't always talk about it.

But it's there.

Sometimes all they want is a little quiet.

A moment to breathe.

A break from noise and conflict.

And sometimes, without meaning to, kids add to the stress.

A fight.

Yelling.

Turning a small problem into a loud one.

In moments like that, it helps to pause.

To ask yourself whether something really needs to be loud right now.

Whether it can wait.

Whether words might work better than explosions.

That pause matters.

Respect often shows up in small ways.

Speaking calmly.

Cleaning up without being asked.

Offering help.

Letting someone else take the first slice.

Getting up to pull out a chair.

Not because you're supposed to.

But because you notice.

Parents remember those moments.

They remember how you made them feel.

Long after grades are forgotten.

Being thoughtful doesn't mean ignoring your own feelings.

It means understanding that you're not the only one
    in the room.

That your actions affect the people around you.

That awareness is a kind of strength.

Your parents are trying.

Even when they're tired.

Even when they get things wrong.

Even when they don't explain themselves very well.

They're learning too.

You don't need to carry their stress.

You don't need to be perfect.

You don't need to make them proud every day.

But noticing them.

Respecting them.

Showing effort.

Those things build trust.

And trust changes things.

Conversations feel easier.

Freedom grows.

Understanding deepens.

School will measure some things.

Life will measure others.

But the way you treat people at home, especially when you don't have to, is one of the things that lasts the longest.

And that's something you get to choose every day.

Chapter 4:
THE SCOREBOARDS EVERYONE PRETENDS NOT TO CARE ABOUT

Almost everywhere you go, there's a scoreboard.

Sometimes it's obvious.

Grades.

Test scores.

Who wins.

Who loses.

Other times it's quieter.

Who gets picked first.

Who people laugh with.

Who gets attention.

Even when no one says anything, you can feel it.

You start noticing where you stand.

And once you notice, it's hard to stop looking.

Scoreboards aren't always bad.

They can make things fun.

They can push you to practice.

They can help you see progress.

The problem starts when the scoreboard becomes
    the whole point.

When winning matters more than learning.

When being liked matters more than being kind.

When not losing matters more than trying.

That's when things start feeling heavy.

Here's something most people don't say out loud.

There's always another scoreboard.

If you win one, another shows up.

If you're good at something, people expect more.

If you're popular, you start worrying about staying popular.

If you get attention, you start worrying about losing it.

The scoreboard never really feels finished.

It just asks for more.

A lot of pressure comes from this.

Not only from school.

Not only from sports.

But from watching yourself all the time.

From quietly asking, "How am I doing compared
    to everyone else?"

That question feels normal.

But it steals your focus.

You've probably seen this happen.

Maybe your friends start making fun of someone.

Nothing huge at first.

Just jokes.

Everyone laughs.

You laugh too, even though something in your
stomach feels weird.

Not because you think it's funny.

But because you don't want to be the one they
turn on next.

In that moment, the scoreboard is running.

And it's asking a hard question.

Do you want the moment to feel safe.

Or do you want to feel proud of yourself later.

No one explains this part.

Small choices shape you.

Not all at once.

Slowly.

You don't notice it happening.

You just start becoming the kind of person who goes along.

Or the kind of person who notices.

The opposite is true too.

Every time you choose what feels right, even when it's
uncomfortable, that also leaves a mark.

You might not get rewarded for it.

You might feel awkward.

But something inside you gets stronger.

You start trusting yourself.

And that trust is hard to break later.

Scoreboards are loud.

Doing what feels right is quiet.

Most people don't notice when you don't join in.

Most people don't say anything when you choose
to be kind.

But you notice.

And you live with that feeling long after the
moment is over.

This doesn't mean you never compete.

It doesn't mean you stop caring.

It means you decide what you're measuring.

Are you measuring yourself by winning.

By being liked.

By never making mistakes.

Or by effort.

By honesty.

By how you treat people when it would be easier not to.

You don't have to be perfect at this.

No one is.

You're going to mess it up sometimes.

Everyone does.

What matters is noticing.

Noticing when you're chasing approval.

Noticing when you're shrinking yourself to fit in.

Noticing when the scoreboard is pulling you away from who you want to be.

Scoreboards are everywhere.

But they don't get to decide who you are.

You get to choose what counts.

And when you do, life starts to feel more like something you're living on your own terms.

Chapter 5:
FITTING IN AND BELONGING AREN'T THE SAME THING

Most kids want the same thing.

They want to belong.

Not to be popular.

Just not to feel alone.

To feel like there's a place where they fit without having to think so hard about it.

Fitting in often feels like the easiest way to get there.

You notice what other kids like.

What they laugh at.

What they make fun of.

Without planning to, you adjust.

You laugh at the same jokes.

You act a little different.

You keep some thoughts to yourself.

At first, it works.

But fitting in takes effort.

You stay alert.

You watch reactions.

You check yourself before you speak.

You make sure you don't stand out in the wrong way.

Even if no one says anything, it uses energy.

Belonging feels different.

It's calmer.

It's when you don't have to disappear to stay included.

It's when you can say what you actually think without
   your stomach tightening.

It's when silence doesn't feel dangerous.

Belonging doesn't mean everyone likes you.

It means the people who matter do.

Sometimes that's fewer people than you expected.

This part can be hard to accept.

Not everyone is meant to be your friend.

That doesn't mean you failed.

It means people connect in different ways.

Some kids bond over sports.

Some over games.

Some over jokes.

Some over being quiet together.

You don't have to force yourself into places that
   don't feel right.

School gives you a lot of chances to learn this.

Recess.

Lunch.

Group projects.

Team games.

Each one shows you something about how it feels to be
    yourself around others.

Sometimes it goes well.

Sometimes it doesn't.

Both teach you something.

You might try sitting with new kids and feel ignored.

You might join a game and not get picked.

You might say something you thought was funny and
    no one laughs.

Those moments hurt.

They can make you want to stop trying.

To stay where it's familiar.

To avoid feeling awkward again.

That reaction makes sense.

But those moments aren't proof that you
    don't belong anywhere.

They're clues.

They show you where you feel comfortable.

And where you don't.

A lot of kids stop trying new things because they don't
want to feel embarrassed.

Embarrassment feels big when it happens.

But it doesn't last.

Regret usually sticks around longer.

Trying something and having it not work out
can feel uncomfortable.

Never trying slowly makes your world smaller.

Belonging usually grows slowly.

In small moments.

A shared look.

A quiet joke.

Sitting next to the same person again.

It builds when you're not forcing it.

If you have to pretend to be someone else to stay included,
that place isn't really yours.

And if you feel relaxed being yourself around someone,
even just one person, that matters more than being liked
by a lot of people.

You don't need to rush this.

You don't need to have friendships figured out right away.

You're allowed to try.

You're allowed to be awkward.

You're allowed to change.

School gives you time to practice all of that.

And the more you learn the difference between fitting in and belonging, the easier it gets to find people who like you for who you actually are.

Not the version you think you're supposed to be.

Chapter 6:
THE SHORTCUT THAT LOOKS EASY

There are moments when you know what feels right.

And moments when you know what doesn't.

Most of the time, those moments
    don't announce themselves.

They just show up.

Maybe you're with a group and someone starts
    getting picked on.

Nothing extreme.

Just comments.

Just jokes.

Everyone's laughing.

You feel that small twist in your stomach.

You recognize it.

You don't stop to think about it.

You react.

You laugh too.

Or you stay quiet.

Or you look away and pretend you didn't hear it.

In that moment, it feels like the easiest choice.

And it works.

You don't get called out.

No one turns on you.

You stay where you are.

Safe.

Included.

That's why it feels like a shortcut.

It gets you through the moment.

What it doesn't show you is what comes after.

Later, when things are quiet, that moment
  sometimes comes back.

Not as a big thought.

Just as a small uncomfortable feeling.

Like something didn't sit right.

You might push it away.

You might tell yourself it wasn't a big deal.

You might say it was just a joke.

But your body remembers.

It remembers how it felt to ignore that signal.

And each time that happens, your brain learns something.

It learns that it's easier not to notice.

There's another option.

It doesn't have to be loud.

It doesn't have to turn into a scene.

Sometimes it's as small as not laughing.

Sometimes it's changing the subject.

Sometimes it's standing next to the person instead
   of joining in.

Those choices don't always feel good either.

They can feel awkward.

They can feel lonely.

They can feel like you just made things harder for yourself.

But later, they feel different.

There isn't that twist.

There isn't that sinking feeling.

There's a quiet sense that you didn't disappear.

A lot of kids think confidence comes from being fearless.

It doesn't.

Confidence comes from knowing you didn't trade yourself
   away to make a moment easier.

That kind of confidence doesn't show off.

But it lasts.

This isn't about always doing the "right" thing.

No one does.

You're going to take shortcuts sometimes.

Everyone does.

What matters is noticing how each choice feels afterward.

Not what other people thought.

Not what happened on the outside.

What happened inside you.

School gives you many chances to notice this.

Every day, there are small moments where you choose
    comfort or honesty.

Most people don't even realize they're choosing.

They just repeat the same patterns.

When you start paying attention, something changes.

You don't suddenly become perfect.

But you feel more solid.

More like yourself.

Like you're standing on your own feet, even when
    things are uncomfortable.

That's how integrity really starts.

Not as a big decision.

But as small moments you begin to notice.

And slowly choose differently.

Chapter 7:
WHY SOME KIDS USE MEANNESS TO FEEL STRONG

You might have noticed this.

Some kids are loud.

Not just loud, but mean.

They tease.

They point things out.

They make comments that don't really feel like jokes.

And somehow, other kids listen.

That can be confusing.

If someone is being mean, why do people laugh?

Why do they follow?

Why does it sometimes seem like the mean kid has power?

Here's what's happening underneath.

Meanness is a fast way to feel important.

When someone puts another person down, they feel bigger for a moment.

When other people react, that feeling gets stronger.

It feels like control.

Like attention.

Like being on top.

That feeling doesn't last.

So it has to be repeated.

The comments get meaner.

The jokes go further.

The behavior gets louder.

Most kids who act this way aren't confident.

They're unsure.

They're worried about being ignored.

They're scared of being the next target.

Meanness feels like armor.

Understanding this doesn't excuse it.

And it doesn't mean you feel sorry for them.

It just means you see what's really going on.

And seeing that gives you choices.

One choice is joining in.

That gives you short-term safety.

It keeps attention off you.

But it also teaches you something about yourself.

The same lesson you noticed in the last chapter.

Another choice is disappearing.

Staying quiet.

Staying small.

Hoping it passes.

Sometimes that's the safest option in the moment.

And that's okay.

There's another option too.

You don't have to fight.

You don't have to win.

You don't have to make a speech.

You can stay where you are and not feed it.

You don't laugh.

You don't pile on.

You don't react the way it expects.

Mean behavior feeds on reaction.

On laughter.

On fear.

On silence that feels like agreement.

When it doesn't get that, it loses energy.

Not instantly.

But over time.

You might notice something else.

Kids who act this way usually don't target everyone.

They choose people who seem unsure.

People who are different.

People who look like they won't push back.

That's not because those kids are weak.

It's because they're human.

If you're ever the one being picked on, there's something
important to remember.

It's not happening because there's something
wrong with you.

It's happening because someone else is trying to feel strong.

That doesn't make it hurt less.

But it changes what it means.

School is one of the first places where you see this
kind of power.

It won't be the last.

People use it in different ways as they get older.

But it always comes from the same place.

Insecurity.

Fear.

Wanting to feel important.

When you understand that, something changes.

Meanness stops feeling mysterious.

It stops feeling personal.

And it stops feeling like something you need to become in
order to survive.

You don't have to prove you're strong by making someone else feel small.

Real strength doesn't work that way.

It doesn't shout.

It doesn't need an audience.

It shows up quietly, in how you treat people when you could get away with being unkind.

Understanding this won't make school perfect.

You'll still run into mean behavior.

You'll still have hard days.

But you'll stop confusing loudness with strength.

And once you stop doing that, meanness starts losing its grip on you too.

Chapter 8:
WHEN YOU'RE THE ONE BEING PICKED ON

Being picked on feels different than watching it happen.

When it's happening to you, your body notices first.

Your stomach tightens.

Your chest feels heavy.

Your thoughts get loud all at once.

You might freeze.

You might want to disappear.

A lot of kids think they're supposed to know what to
    do right away.

Say the perfect thing.

Be confident.

Act like it doesn't matter.

But most people don't feel like that in the moment.

They feel stuck.

One of the hardest parts is what your mind
    starts telling you.

Maybe they're right.

Maybe there's something wrong with me.

Maybe if I were different, this wouldn't be happening.

Those thoughts can feel very real when you're
    alone with them.

But they aren't the truth.

What's happening isn't about you being weak.

It's about someone else trying to feel strong.

That doesn't take away the hurt.

But it changes what the moment means.

A lot of advice about bullying sounds simple.

Ignore it.

Stand up for yourself.

Tell an adult.

Sometimes those things help.

Sometimes they don't.

What matters most is knowing you're allowed
    to protect yourself.

Protecting yourself doesn't always mean fighting back.

Sometimes it means getting help, even if
    that feels uncomfortable.

Sometimes it means staying close to people who feel safe.

Sometimes it means walking away instead of reacting.

Sometimes it means saying, "That's not okay," and leaving.

You don't have to handle everything on your own.

That idea sounds strong, but it makes things harder.

Talking to someone you trust doesn't mean you failed.

It means you're taking care of yourself.

There's another part that doesn't get talked about much.

Being picked on can make you feel embarrassed.

Like you should have handled it better.

Like other people would think less of you if they knew.

That shame can feel heavier than the teasing itself.

Here's the truth.

Nothing about being picked on means you deserved it.

Nothing about it means you're weak.

It means you were in a tough situation
    without much control.

Anyone would struggle with that.

Over time, moments like this teach
    you something important.

They teach you what kind of treatment you don't accept.

They teach you how much kindness matters.

They teach you how strong you can be, even when you
    don't feel brave.

What happened still wasn't okay.

But it doesn't get to define you.

One day, this will be a memory.

Not who you are.

If you're going through something like this right
now, remember this.

You are not broken.

You are not alone.

And this moment, as big as it feels, is not the end
of your story.

Chapter 9:
WHEN YOUR FEELINGS ALL SHOW UP AT ONCE

Sometimes it isn't one big thing.

It's a bunch of small things that pile up.

A comment.

A bad grade.

Someone not texting back.

A strange look.

Nothing huge on its own.

But together, they feel like too much.

When that happens, your feelings don't line up neatly.

They all arrive at the same time.

Anger.

Sadness.

Embarrassment.

Worry.

They overlap and get loud.

It can make you wonder if something is wrong with you.

A lot of kids think they're supposed to
    control their feelings.

Like if you're upset, you should calm down.

If you're nervous, you should stop worrying.

If you're sad, you should cheer up.

But feelings don't work that way.

They don't follow instructions.

Feelings are more like waves.

They rise.

They peak.

They fall.

Even the big ones.

Even the uncomfortable ones.

The trouble starts when you think the wave is going
    to stay forever.

When emotions hit all at once, your thoughts
    usually join in.

They tell stories.

This always happens to me.

I can't handle this.

Everyone else is fine except me.

Those thoughts feel convincing when your
    feelings are loud.

But they aren't facts.

They're just thoughts riding along.

You don't have to make feelings go away for them to pass.

You don't have to fix them.

You don't have to understand them right away.

Most of the time, they settle on their own if you
    don't fight them.

That doesn't mean ignoring them.

It means noticing them.

You might think, "This feels like too much right now."

Not, "I'm weak."

Just noticing the difference can help more
    than you'd expect.

Sometimes the most helpful thing you can do is slow
    your body down.

Take a breath that's a little longer than usual.

Put your feet on the ground.

Look around and name a few things you can see.

Not to make the feeling disappear.

Just to remind yourself that you're here.

And that you're safe.

Big feelings don't mean you're bad at life.

They usually mean you care.

They mean something matters to you.

That's not a problem.

Everyone you know has moments like this.

Some hide it better.

Some don't talk about it.

But no one feels calm all the time.

And no one expects you to.

Over time, you start to learn your own patterns.

What sets you off.

What helps you settle.

What makes things worse.

That knowledge gives you confidence.

It helps you trust yourself more.

Feelings don't control you.

They visit.

Sometimes they stay longer than you want.

But they always move on.

Even the heavy ones.

You don't need to rush yourself through them.

You don't need to judge yourself for having them.

You're learning how to feel and still keep going.

That's part of growing up.

Chapter 10:

WHEN YOUR BRAIN WON'T STOP TALKING

Sometimes the problem isn't how you feel.

It's what your brain keeps saying.

It talks when you're trying to sleep.

It talks when you're trying to focus.

It brings things back up that already happened.

It worries about things that haven't happened yet.

And it doesn't wait for permission.

A lot of kids think something is wrong with them
  because of this.

They wonder why they can't just stop thinking.

But a busy mind doesn't mean a broken one.

It means your brain is active.

Your brain is always looking ahead.

It searches for problems.

It imagines what could go wrong.

It replays moments to see if it missed something.

Sometimes that's helpful.

Sometimes it's just loud.

The tricky part is that your brain sends every thought the same way.

Helpful ones.

Unhelpful ones.

Scary ones.

Random ones.

And if you treat all of them like facts, things can start to feel like too much, really fast.

Here's something worth remembering.

Just because a thought shows up doesn't mean it's true.

And just because it sounds serious doesn't mean you have to act on it.

Thoughts are more like pop-ups.

They appear.

They try to grab your attention.

But you don't have to click.

When your mind says things like "What if this goes wrong?" or "Everyone is judging me" or "I'm going to mess this up," it feels urgent.

Like you need to fix something right now.

But most of the time, those thoughts are guesses.

Not warnings.

You don't need to argue with them.

You don't need to push them away.

That usually makes them louder.

Instead, you can notice them.

"Oh. There's that thought again."

Not annoyed.

Just aware.

When you notice a thought instead of getting pulled into
it, something changes.

There's a little space.

You're not stuck inside it anymore.

You're watching it pass.

And thoughts don't have as much power when
you're watching them.

This takes practice.

You'll forget.

You'll get pulled in again.

That's normal.

Noticing after the fact still counts.

Each time you notice, you're learning.

Sometimes it helps to bring your attention
to something steady.

Your breathing.

The feeling of your feet on the floor.

The sounds around you.

Not to make thoughts disappear.

Just to give your mind somewhere to rest.

A calm mind doesn't mean no thoughts.

It means the thoughts aren't running everything.

They're just part of the background.

Everyone has a brain that talks too much sometimes.

Some people just pretend they don't.

Learning how to listen without obeying is a skill.

And life gives you plenty of chances to practice it.

You are not your thoughts.

You're the one noticing them.

And that's a much quieter place to stand.

Chapter 11:
BEING ALONE DOESN'T HAVE TO MEAN BEING LONELY

A lot of kids don't like being alone.

Not because they need people all the time.

But because being alone can feel strange.

Quiet.

Like there's nowhere to hide.

When no one else is around, your thoughts get louder.

You notice things about yourself.

What you're feeling.

What you're thinking.

What you wish were different.

That can feel uncomfortable if you're not used to it.

Loneliness isn't really about being by yourself.

It's about feeling disconnected.

You can feel lonely in a crowded room.

And you can feel calm when you're alone.

The difference isn't who's nearby.

It's how you feel with yourself.

Some kids fill every quiet moment.

They grab a screen.

They look for noise.

They distract themselves.

Not because they're doing something wrong.

But because silence feels unfamiliar.

Boredom gets treated like a problem.

Like something to escape.

But boredom is often the moment right before
    curiosity shows up.

It's the space where your mind starts to wander.

Starts to imagine.

Starts to notice what you actually care about.

When there's always noise around you, you don't get
    to hear yourself.

You don't learn what you like when no one is watching.

You don't learn what you think when no one
    answers for you.

Being alone gives you that chance.

You'll still want friends.

You'll still care about people.

You're just not depending on them to feel okay.

You're learning how to be steady on your own.

Being comfortable alone is a quiet kind of confidence.

It doesn't show off.

It doesn't need attention.

It just feels solid.

Like you're not rushing to be somewhere else.

At first, being alone might feel awkward.

You might feel restless.

You might feel bored.

You might feel like you should be doing something.

That's normal.

If you don't run from it, it starts to ease.

Over time, you start enjoying small things.

Drawing.

Thinking.

Listening to music.

Walking.

Doing nothing for a bit.

Those moments help you recharge.

People who are okay being alone often choose
    friends more carefully.

They don't need everyone to like them.

They don't stay in places that don't feel right just to avoid
being by themselves.

They know they'll be okay either way.

You don't need to become someone who's alone
all the time.

You just need to know you can handle it.

That you're good company for yourself.

That you don't disappear when things get quiet.

Learning how to be alone without feeling lonely is like
building a strong base.

Everything else sits on top of it.

Friendships.

Confidence.

Choices.

And once you have that base, the world feels like a lot
less to handle.

Because no matter what's happening around you, you
know you can come back to yourself.

And be okay there.

Chapter 12:
WINNING, LOSING, AND TRYING NOT TO LET IT DECIDE YOU

Competition shows up pretty early.

Games.

Sports.

Grades.

Contests.

Sometimes it's fun.

Sometimes it feels like everything.

Winning feels good.

There's nothing wrong with that.

You feel proud.

You feel excited.

You feel like the work paid off.

That feeling is real.

Losing feels bad.

That's real too.

Your chest tightens.

Your face gets hot.

You might feel embarrassed.

You might feel angry.

You might feel like quitting.

A lot of kids think the goal is to stop caring about winning and losing.

That's not really the point.

The point is to care without letting it take over.

Trouble starts when winning turns into proof.

Proof that you're good enough.

Proof that you're better than others.

Proof that you matter.

When that happens, losing starts to feel dangerous.

Like it says something about who you are.

You can see this in sports.

You miss a shot.

You make a mistake.

Suddenly you're not having fun anymore.

You're just trying not to mess up again.

Your body gets tight.

Your thoughts get loud.

The same thing can happen in school.

One bad grade can feel huge.

Like it cancels out all the good ones.

Like it changes how smart you think you are.

Even when part of you knows that doesn't make sense.

Here's something worth remembering.

Winning and losing are events.

They happen.

And then they're over.

They don't get to decide who you are unless you let them.

There's a difference between trying to win and
needing to win.

Trying to win means you care about doing your best.

Needing to win means you're scared of what it means
if you don't.

That fear drains the fun out of things.

Some kids stop trying new things because they're
afraid of losing.

They don't join teams.

They don't raise their hand.

They don't try unless they think they'll be good right away.

That's a quiet loss too.

Being a beginner can feel uncomfortable.

You don't know what you're doing yet.

You mess up more than you succeed.

Other people might be better than you.

That's part of learning.

Everyone you admire was bad at something once.

They just stayed long enough to improve.

Not because they never lost.

But because they didn't let losing make them stop.

Losing can teach you things winning never does.

It shows you where you can grow.

It shows you how you handle disappointment.

It shows you whether you quit or keep going.

You don't have to like losing.

No one does.

Just don't let it shrink you.

Let it teach you.

Some of the strongest people aren't the ones who
win the most.

They're the ones who can lose and still show up
the next time.

Without excuses.

Without blaming.

Without giving up.

Competition can be a good teacher.

But only if you remember this.

You are more than the result.

You were someone before the game.

You're someone after the game.

And one moment doesn't get to erase that.

Chapter 13:
LOOKING SIDEWAYS CAN MAKE YOU MISS YOUR OWN PATH

It's hard not to compare yourself to other people.

You notice who's faster.

Who's better.

Who gets more attention.

Who seems more confident.

Sometimes it happens without you trying.

Comparison can feel useful at first.

It shows you what's possible.

It tells you where you stand.

It can even push you to try harder.

But it has a way of sticking around longer than it should.

When you spend too much time looking
     sideways, something changes.

You stop noticing your own progress.

Small wins don't feel like much anymore.

You start measuring yourself by things you can't control.

You might see someone who's better than you at something and think, "I'll never catch up."

You might see someone who's struggling and think, "At least I'm not them."

Neither thought feels good for long.

Comparison has a trick.

It never shows you the whole picture.

You only see the outside.

You don't see how long they practiced.

You don't see what they worry about.

You don't see what's hard for them.

When you compare yourself to someone else, you're usually comparing your inside to their outside.

That was never a fair comparison.

It was never meant to be.

Your path can't look like anyone else's.

You have different interests.

Different strengths.

Different timing.

Trying to follow someone else's path will only wear you out.

Growth doesn't move in straight lines.

Some days you feel ahead.

Some days you feel behind.

Most days, you're moving forward in ways you won't
  notice until later.

When comparison takes over, you forget why you started.

You forget what you enjoy.

You forget what you're curious about.

You forget what progress feels like for you.

There's a better way to measure things.

You can look back instead of sideways.

You can ask, "Am I better than I was?"

"Did I try today?"

"Did I learn something new?"

Those questions don't shout.

But they tell the truth.

This doesn't mean you never notice other people.

It means you stop using them as a ruler.

They're walking their own path.

You're walking yours.

Both can exist at the same time.

When you stop looking sideways so much,
  something surprising happens.

You feel lighter.

You feel more focused.

You feel more like yourself again.

Your path won't always make sense to other people.

That's okay.

It only has to make sense to you.

And the more attention you give to your own steps, the
easier it gets to keep going.

Chapter 14:
WHAT PEOPLE THINK WILL MAKE THEM HAPPY

As you grow up, you start hearing the same ideas again and again.

Do well in school.

Be successful.

Make money.

Be important.

People talk about these things like they're the finish line.

Like once you get there, everything feels good.

It makes sense that kids notice this.

You see who gets attention.

You see who's popular.

You see who has the newest stuff.

It's easy to think, "If I had that, I'd feel better."

A lot of adults think that too.

Getting what you want does feel good.

At least at first.

There's excitement.

There's relief.

There's pride.

But the feeling fades.

Then something else takes its place.

Something newer.

Something bigger.

Something more.

This doesn't make money bad.

And it doesn't mean success doesn't matter.

Those things can make life easier.

They can give you options.

They can help you take care of yourself and other people.

But they don't do the job people expect them to do.

They don't make everything feel okay inside.

Some people spend their whole lives chasing that feeling.

They think the next win will finally fix it.

The next upgrade.

The next level.

But the feeling never stays.

What lasts is how you live.

How you treat people.

How you treat yourself.

Whether you feel comfortable with who you are when
    things are quiet.

You've probably noticed this already.

Some people have a lot and still seem unhappy.

Some people don't have much and still seem okay.

That's not random.

The things that last aren't loud.

They don't show off.

They don't get posted everywhere.

They're things like trust.

Curiosity.

Respect.

Being able to sleep at night without your thoughts racing.

When you build your life around things that fade quickly,
    you end up feeling like you're always chasing.

When you build it around things that last, you
    feel more grounded.

Even when life gets messy.

This doesn't mean you stop wanting things.

It means you don't expect them to do more than they can.

You let achievements be achievements.

Not proof that you matter.

People who seem the most at peace aren't usually the ones
    who won the most.

They're the ones who know what matters to them.

And live in a way that matches it.

You don't have to figure all of this out now.

You're not supposed to.

Just noticing that there's more than one way to measure a
good life is enough for now.

That idea will grow with you.

One day, when you're deciding what to chase,
you'll remember this.

You'll remember that happiness isn't something you earn
once and keep forever.

It's something you build quietly, over time, with the choices
you make each day.

Chapter 15:
THE KIND OF PERSON LIFE LISTENS TO

Some people walk into a room and get attention right away.

They're loud.

They're confident.

They seem important.

Other people don't stand out like that.

But when they speak, people listen.

You've probably met someone like this.

They don't show off.

They don't try to impress everyone.

They're solid.

You feel like you can trust them, even if you can't explain why.

That kind of presence doesn't come from winning.

It doesn't come from popularity.

It comes from character.

Character shows up when no one is watching.

It's what you do when there's nothing to gain.

It's how you act when honesty would be easier to avoid.

Most people don't think about character very often.

They focus on results.

Did I win?

Did I get noticed?

Did I get what I wanted?

But results change.

Character stays.

You build character in small moments.

In how you treat someone who can't do anything for you.

In whether you keep a promise you made to yourself.

In whether you tell the truth when it would be easier not to.

Those moments don't feel important
    while they're happening.

No one claps.

No one keeps score.

Sometimes no one even notices.

But they add up anyway.

Life responds to this over time.

Not all at once.

Not in obvious ways.

People begin to trust you.

They take you seriously.

They want you around.

This doesn't mean life is always fair.

Good people still struggle.

Doing the right thing doesn't protect you from hard days.

But it protects something else.

Your relationship with yourself.

When your actions match what you believe, you feel solid.

You don't replay things over and over.

You don't second-guess yourself as much.

You know where you stand.

That kind of self-trust makes other things easier.

Friendships.

Decisions.

Walking away when something doesn't feel right.

Standing up for yourself when it matters.

Character isn't about being perfect.

It's about noticing when you aren't.

And choosing to do better next time.

Everyone messes up.

Everyone makes choices they wish they could change.

What matters is whether you learn from them.

Or pretend they didn't matter.

The world has plenty of people trying to look important.

It's quieter around people who actually are.

Those are the people life listens to.

Not because they demand it.

But because they've earned it.

You're building that kind of person already.

Every day.

In small ways.

Whether you realize it or not.

Chapter 16:
WHEN THINGS AREN'T FAIR

At some point, every kid notices this.

Things aren't fair.

Someone works hard and still loses.

Someone else barely tries and still wins.

Kind people get treated badly.

Mean people get away with things.

And no one explains why.

When you're younger, adults sometimes say things like "It will even out" or "Life is fair in the end."

They usually mean well.

But that isn't always how things work.

And pretending it is can make things feel worse.

Life doesn't hand out rewards based on effort alone.

It never has.

Some people start ahead.

Some start behind.

Some get lucky.

Some don't.

That's not something you caused.

And it's not something you can always change.

This can feel confusing.

You might wonder what the point of trying is if things
    don't always work out.

That question makes sense.

A lot of people quietly give up right there.

But unfairness doesn't decide who you become.

How you respond to it does.

You can't control whether things are fair.

But you can choose what unfairness turns you into.

Whether it makes you bitter.

Whether it makes you cruel.

Whether it convinces you nothing matters.

Some people use unfairness as an excuse.

They stop trying.

They stop caring.

They decide the world owes them something.

That path doesn't lead anywhere good.

Other people notice the unfairness.

They don't like it.

But they keep going anyway.

They learn how to adapt.

They learn how to stay kind without being
taken advantage of.

They learn how to keep their self-respect even when things
don't go their way.

Those people aren't lucky.

They know how to keep going.

And knowing how to keep going lasts longer than
fairness ever could.

There's another hard truth.

Sometimes you can do everything right and still lose.

That doesn't mean your effort was wasted.

It means effort changes you, even when it doesn't
change what happens.

The world will never be perfectly fair.

But it does respond to certain things over time.

Consistency.

Honesty.

Adaptability.

The ability to keep going without losing yourself.

That's why school, friendships, and hard moments matter.

They're not preparing you for a fair world.

They're preparing you for a real one.

You don't need to like unfairness.

No one does.

You just need to understand that it's part of the game.

And that you still get to decide how you play.

Some days that choice feels easy.

Some days it doesn't.

But every time you choose to keep your values in an unfair
    moment, you get stronger.

Even if no one notices.

Even if nothing changes right away.

Life doesn't promise fairness.

But it does offer something else.

The chance to become someone you respect.

Even when things don't go your way.

Chapter 17:
SOME KIDS START IN DIFFERENT PLACES

At some point, most kids notice this too.

Not everyone's life looks the same.

Some kids have bigger houses.

Some have nicer things.

Some go on trips.

Some don't.

Some parents seem calm.

Some seem stressed all the time.

It's easy to start wondering what that means.

Why their life looks easier.

Why your family feels different.

Whether something about you or your home is wrong.

Those thoughts can slip in quietly.

Here's what helps to understand.

Families start in different places.

They have different money situations.

Different pressures.

Different histories.

Different problems they're dealing with.

That doesn't make one family better than another.

It just means life handed out different starting points.

Kids don't get to choose where they begin.

You don't choose how much money your family has.

You don't choose what your parents are carrying.

You don't choose what happens behind closed doors.

None of that says anything about your worth.

Sometimes kids feel embarrassed about things
    they shouldn't be.

Not having the newest stuff.

Not being able to do everything other kids do.

Living somewhere smaller.

Having parents who worry a lot.

Those things can feel big when you're comparing.

But appearances don't tell the full story.

Every family is carrying something.

You just don't always get to see it.

Some kids learn independence early.

Some learn responsibility early.

Some learn empathy early.

Some learn patience the hard way.

Those lessons count too.

They just don't always get noticed right away.

It's not fair that some kids have it easier.

And it's okay to feel upset about that.

Feeling that way doesn't make you ungrateful.

It makes you honest.

What matters most isn't where you start.

It's what you learn along the way.

How you adapt.

How you treat people.

How you take care of yourself when things feel hard.

Your circumstances aren't the end of your story.

They're a starting point.

And starting points don't decide endings.

One day, you'll look back and realize something.

The things you thought made you "less than" taught you
     how to stand on your own.

How to notice others.

How to keep going.

Those lessons stay with you.

You don't need to be ashamed of where you come from.

You don't need to hide it.

You don't need to compare it.

Your story is still unfolding.

And it matters.

Chapter 18:
YOU'RE ALLOWED TO BE A WORK IN PROGRESS

By now, you've probably noticed something.

Growing up isn't about getting everything right.

It's about learning how to keep going when things don't turn out the way you expected.

You're going to mess up.

You're going to feel unsure.

You're going to make choices you're proud of.

And some you wish you could change.

That's not a failure.

That's how becoming yourself actually works.

A lot of people think confidence means having no doubts.

It doesn't.

Confidence is knowing that even when you doubt yourself, you can handle it.

That you don't disappear when things feel uncomfortable.

That you don't stop being you when life gets hard.

You don't have to rush.

You don't have to become someone impressive right away.

You don't have to prove anything to anyone.

You're allowed to grow at your own pace.

Some days you'll feel strong.

Some days you won't.

Some days things will make sense.

Some days they won't.

None of those days cancel the others out.

They all count.

The world will keep offering you scoreboards.

It will keep trying to tell you what matters.

You don't have to listen to all of it.

You get to decide what kind of person you want to be.

And you get to practice that choice every day.

You're not behind.

You're not broken.

You're not missing something everyone else has.

You're learning.

Just like everyone else.

If there's one thing to hold on to, it's this.

You don't need to be finished to be enough.

You don't need to have everything figured out to
    be doing okay.

You don't need to know who you'll become to be on
the right path.

Life isn't asking you to be perfect.

It's asking you to be honest.

Curious.

Willing to try again.

And if you can do that, even on the days when it feels hard,
you're already doing better than you think.

You're becoming someone you can respect.

One step at a time.